MY
LIFE'S
JOURNEY

MY
LIFE'S
JOURNEY

TIM CRONIN

ARPress
ILLUMINATING IDEAS
EMPOWERING VOICES

ARPress
45 Dan Road Suite 5
Canton MA 02021

Hotline: 1(800) 220-7660
Fax: 1(855) 752-6001

Ordering Information:
Quantity sales. Special discounts are available on quantity purchases by corporations, associations, and others. For details, contact the publisher at the address above.

Printed in the United States of America.

| ISBN-13: | Paperback | 979-8-89389-717-3 |
| | eBook | 979-8-89389-718-0 |

Library of Congress Control Number: 2021909590

CONTENTS

INTRODUCTION

The following story consists of different events that have occurred throughout my life. It starts with my childhood, being diagnosed with a form of autism at an early age, dealing with it growing up, and ending with where I'm at now. My reason for writing this book is to reach out to people that have any form of autism. It's not easy being different from other individuals that aren't autistic. It teaches friends, family, and others to have patience and understanding. If it wasn't for certain people in my life helping and guiding me, I wouldn't be where I'm at today. Just because you have some sort of learning disability, it doesn't mean that we should be discouraged or frustrated to learn or try new things.

PART 1

MY CHILDHOOD AND SCHOOL YEARS

My story begins on July 9, 1984. I was born in Pittsburgh, Pennsylvania at Magee Women's Hospital. My parents, Janet, and Patrick Cronin, owned a house in a small borough called Trafford, PA where I grew up. Aside from my parents I also have a sister, Andrea, who is four years older than me. The wonderful thing about Trafford being so small was that everyone knew everyone.

Growing up I wasn't a normal kid. There were some signs that I was different than other kids my age or around my age. For example, my parents would interact with me and a lot of times I wouldn't respond to them because I had developmental delays with both speech and language. Also I had a short attention span doing certain activities and would flap my hands and make odd noises. On June 5, 1989, I was diagnosed with a form of autism known as pervasive developmental disorder. That helped put things into perspective as to why my behavior was strange. Before that, I was enrolled in Trinity preschool from September to November 1988. Due to my disability, I didn't fit well into the program at that preschool. While I was there, I attended two days a week from 9:30 to 11:30 AM. On the Stanford Binet IV test, in the vocabulary portion, I really struggled with being able to show the teacher certain items in a picture. Also I would be very uncooperative and wouldn't attempt to complete any tasks that were given to me, so my Mom would have to help me with them. All of these factors combined made my parents hired an aide to help me through the process.

In 1989, due to all the difficulties that I was having at the other preschool, I ended up attending another one at Mt. View Elementary in Greensburg, PA. The teacher's name was Janis Panichella. Even though I was attending a different school that could give me better help, my behavior was still the same with the hand wringing, flapping, and the odd noises. Janice could conform to my needs, such as slowing down on certain lessons so that I could understand them better. The teacher utilized a behavior modification program to help eliminate my inappropriate behaviors and speech. I was given five sticks or rods in a can daily. The way I was able to earn the sticks was by listening, sitting quietly, interacting appropriately with peers, complying with adults wishes, and answering questions to the best of my ability. If I acted inappropriately with objects, made odd noises, and did my hand ringing or flapping then all my sticks would be taken away and therefore I wouldn't be able to participate in free time while the rest of my peers did. This would motivate me to behave better because I would become very sad and cry most of the time.

During my school year of 1991, I went to speech sessions with the speech language therapist James Matta. He was great at helping me improve my speech skills during my time at elementary school. After finishing preschool, I was enrolled at Level Green Elementary instead of Trafford Elementary, which was closer to me, because I could continue getting the help, I needed to improve my education skills. By the end of the 1992-93 school year, I'd shown an improvement in my speech skills and could start communicating better with people.

The summers of 1993 and 1994 were spent playing Little League. The first year I played for the Royals followed by playing for the Indians during my last year. It was a fun activity. Whenever it was my turn to bat, it would be very difficult for me to hit the ball within three tries and would strike out half the time. One evening, my family and I drove up to the Middle School to practice hitting the ball. For some reason that night didn't help. I got very frustrated and was crying at one point. My parents told me to just keep practicing and be patient. Eventually it paid off and I didn't strike out as much. My mom, who was a stay-at-home mom, would drive me to school and I would take the bus home. While I was in school, my dad taught engineering at Penn State University. The number one subject that I struggled with in school was math. My dad was good at that subject so whenever I was having a tough time with it, he always helped me out throughout my school years. An example of my odd behavior was one day I walked to throw my lunch away in the school cafeteria. Out of nowhere, I did my arm flapping and said the word, "wahhh" at the same time in front of all the students. Truth be told, I was trying to imitate the Headless Horsemen's laugh from the *Legend of Sleepy Hollow* cartoon and instead did the other thing.

In first grade, my teacher Don Mortimore also did some one-on-one activities to help me out with better understanding certain school subjects and activities. That was the same year that I met my best friend, Ryan Oreski. At first he and I didn't get along, him and three other guys, John, Josh, and Frank, gave me a tough time and picked on me. That year was when I learned about professional wrestling on T.V. One day during class, Josh threw names out at me like Hulk Hogan, Ted DiBiase, and some other wrestling names then he asked me if I knew who they were. My response was "no". Not too long after that I started watching wrestling on a weekly basis and got into it. My dad and I would go to see the wrestling events in Downtown Pittsburgh at the Civic Arena. Truth be told, whenever we went to the events they really didn't interest me. I liked watching it better on T.V.

A few weeks later, my mom and I were walking in Downtown Trafford and we walked past the house where Ryan and his family lived. He saw me, approached, and said he felt bad for picking on me. He then asked me if we could hang out sometime. I said yes and after that we started hanging out. Eventually, he ended up going to Trafford Elementary a few years later when we were both in fourth grade. Even though he and I were going to two different schools, we kept in touch, which was easy since we both lived in the same area. One night in the summertime, Ryan and I had raced each other, half of the time he was able to outrun me, and, on that night, I ended up winning the race which surprised both of us. A couple of years later, some new neighbors moved in across the street. It was a married couple with three kids, one of them was a couple years younger than me. He introduced himself and said his name was Tim. That same year, I met my friend Chuck Rainey as well. Chuck, Tim, and I hung out a lot during the school year as well as over the summer.

The three of us were also in Cub Scouts together. The same place I went to originally for preschool was where we had our Cub Scout meetings. After that, meetings were held at the Scout Leader's house up the street from where I lived. Towards the end of my Cub Scout years, my parents were the Scout Leaders and our final meetings were held at the Borough Building in Downtown Trafford. Cub Scouts was fun. We did projects to earn pins on our uniforms depending on what the project was. After earning so many badges, everyone went on from Cub Scouts to Boy Scouts. There was a ceremony held in which there was a little bridge that the Cub Scouts would cross, symbolizing the transition from Cub to Boy Scouts. One summer, my dad and I went to Cub Scout Camp which was fun. We went swimming, hiking, and other activities. Each parent and child got a tent together, which they helped build.

During the summertime, my parents, sister, and I would drive to Rehoboth Beach in Delaware to meet up with my relatives from New Jersey, my three cousins, Sarah, Kaitlyn, and Will, as well as my Uncle Bill and Aunt Lauren. That was always a great trip and I looked forward to going each time. Another trip my family and I would take each summer was to North Carolina to visit my Grandma Cronin, my dad's mom. I would ask the age-old question, "Are we there yet?" Instead of just saying "no," my dad came up with a response of his own by saying, "we must go up a hill, then down a hill, and then go around some bends". To me that was an original and very clever response. The two of us would also go down to North Carolina to visit my Uncle Dan and Aunt Terina and my two cousins Dylan and Katie. My aunt and uncle lived in a house by a lake and my uncle owned a Boat. There were a few times my uncle took us out on the boat. Mainly I would just go swimming in the lake in front of his house.

During the drive down to my aunt and uncle's house with my dad, we would always stay at a Days Inn Hotel in Clarksburg, West Virginia then drive the rest of the way down the next morning. One time my Dad worked late and we didn't end up leaving for our trip until around 5 PM. It was 12 AM and we were about an hour away from the Days Inn we stayed at. My dad was getting tired from driving and spotted a sign for another Days Inn on an exit sign. We got off the exit and went to the front desk. When my Dad asked if there were any rooms available, he was told all the rooms were booked. We got back in the car and drove to the other Days Inn that we always stayed at.

Kennywood and Idlewild were two amusement parks that my family and I would go to every summer. Idlewild was the park that we went to the most when I was a kid, mainly because it was a family park more than Kennywood. Penn Trafford always had their school picnic at Kennywood on the very first Friday of June, at the end of the school year. The fall of the same year in 1995 was the beginning of fourth grade. Mr. Riner was one of my teachers that year and he would tell our class this ghost story about John Crudgon. There were many times that he would start the story however, he never finished it. My math teacher that I had that year was very interesting. He would start to teach class each day and about five minutes into class he would give us our assignment then sit with his feet propped up on the desk and read the newspaper. In reading class, we would have this test occasionally where you would have to read a story and answer questions at the end. The first question was always, "What was the main idea of the story itself?" Unfortunately, that question always puzzled me every single time and couldn't seem to get it right. Math and reading that year were my two hardest subjects and could be very frustrating. I had a remedial teacher for both subjects that could help me better understand the material better and was very helpful.

My final year at Level Green was a very interesting one. In the fall of 1996, Level Green, Trafford, Harrison Park, and some other elementary schools took a trip to Deer Valley. Deer Valley was a lake and campground about two hours away from my school. All the students from the different schools stayed in a cabin with four in one room and in the other was a chaperone. The classmates in my cabin would joke around with me about there being a bed monster and a heater monster. When I told them there's no such thing, they kept insisting there was. During our time there, we would do different activities. During breakfast and lunch time there would be a person that was called the

"Gopher". The Gopher's job was to go to the building we ate at and would help set up the tables. I was a Gopher a few times and really enjoyed it. Other activities we did included learning different dances such as the Electric Slide and the Macarena. We also got to go fishing, one day we did and I caught one. Another day we got to shoot bows and arrows, which was my favorite activity we did. That day I got a bullseye. I couldn't believe it and neither could any one of the teachers that were there. A bunch of the kids started chanting my name and it felt great for both of those things to happen.

At night we had to have the lights out by a certain time, but one night we had the lights on after. David Spudy, the principal of both Trafford Elementary and Middle School was walking around outside and saw the lights in our cabin were still on. He asked, "Is there a problem in there?" We said no and he yelled, "lights out," then walked away. Our last night there we got pizza as our last meal and were told we must sing for our pizza. During the days leading up to that, we learned different songs that we had to sing and that last night we walked in we didn't know which song we would have to sing. Whenever we sat down, the song we had to sing was there in front of us in a booklet already turned to the page number the song was on. "On Top of Spaghetti" was the song we had to sing. The next morning we got on the bus and headed back home. On the ride, these girls were sitting in the back that were sitting in the back were singing the Lamp Chop song from the T.V. show.

In January 1997, my Grandma Cronin passed away so I flew down to North Carolina with my mom and sister to attend the funeral. We were down there for a few days and then came back home. When I came back, I had a bunch of schoolwork to catch up on. Scott Bruggeman, Jeff Coles, Mark Wozinak, and Tyler Okel were the only real friends that I had at school. Scott was the one person that I interacted with the most, even though at times I could really drive him crazy. Mandy

Skutch's dad was taught by my dad at Penn State. I didn't know that until she told me one day.

In the fall at the start my fifth-grade school year, I learned how to play the alto saxophone and joined the band. My dad played the soprano saxophone and clarinet so that influenced me to want to learn a musical instrument. There were times where I would play too loud and upset the band instructor. It was fun playing in the band. At the end of the year, all the fifth graders got yearbooks and prior to getting those everyone filled out a questionnaire. The questions included what your memories were, what famous person you would have lunch with, and what you would be doing in the year 2012. The yearbook also had pictures of all the students with their baby pictures and you had to match the numbers to the students. Elementary school was over. By then I had accomplished a lot and was ready to move on to middle school.

That summer, I took Karate lessons at N.A.K.F. North American Karate and Fitness in Murrysville, which wasn't real far from where my parents lived. My karate instructor was Chuck McFarland, twice a week on Fridays and Saturdays, was when I attended classes. For the red belts and black belts, they had a class of their own on Thursday evenings. Instead of attending Saturday morning classes, I attended the red and black belt class on Thursday evenings. Going to those classes helped me to get better acquainted with the forms that I had to learn and perform. To eventually to receive a black belt, the ranking system went white belt, yellow belt, green belt, red belt, and then black. Tests were taken to move on in rankings, things such as certain forms and breaking boards were part of the tests. Once you got three stripes on your green belt, you moved on to red belt. With the red belt it was four stripes before you could take the black belt test. During the black belt test, you had to take a multiple-choice test consisting of terminology questions, performing a black belt form, defense techniques, and breaking three different boards.

PART 2

TEENAGE YEARS

At the end of summer, a week before starting sixth grade, there was an orientation at Trafford Middle School. Mr. Spudy gave the orientation and it was a very interesting one. He yelled the entire time about different things, mainly about the dress code, and mentioned a few times about how the students had to wear belts and tuck their shirts in. The first day of school he was on the other side of the doors and if you didn't have your shirt tucked in, he would yell at the students and tell them to tuck their shirt in. That only lasted the first day, the next day he made an announcement telling people they no longer had to however, the rest of the dress code rules still applied. During school assemblies and at lunchtime if he wanted to say something, he would put his hand up and use his infamous phrase, "When my hand goes up, your mouths go shut." The big rule at the school was that you didn't want to break was chewing gum. If a teacher caught you doing it, you would get sent to the office and get after-school detention. Mr. Spudy was a good guy and if he didn't know your name that meant you were safe because you never got sent to his office.

My classmates that I met that year were cool. I started making new friends and had my other friends from elementary school there as well. Some people in my grade listened to Heavy Metal music, in particular two bands that I never heard of called Korn and Pantera. My parents wouldn't let me listen those bands or other bands that had the "Parental Advisory" label on it. They objected to it mainly because of the violent content in the songs. I asked my dad when I could listen to that type of music and he told me when I was eighteen. Those weren't good enough reasons in my opinion.

One day after school, my mom, Grandma Riden who was my mom's mother, and I went to the Monroeville Mall. My mom and grandma were looking around at the different stores while I was shopping at the music store Waves for a CD. When I was at Waves, I bought a CD that I wasn't allowed to buy. The CD was *Official Live 101 Proof.* After buying the CD I met up with my mom and grandma. When my mom saw the bag, she asked me what I bought. When I pulled the CD out of the bag, my mom was shocked, her eyes got really big, and she yelled, "Parental Advisory Explicit Content" and then walked into the store to return the CD. After we left the mall on the ride home, my excuse for buying the CD was that it said, "Pure Against the Grain American Metal" but my mom didn't fall for it. When we got back to the house, I was really scared of what my Dad's reaction was going to be. After confessing to what I'd done, to my surprise, my Dad was also shocked however he didn't make a big deal out of it. That little stunt I pulled ended up getting me grounded for a few days. That taught me a lesson and I never did it again.

A few years later, my family and I were opening gifts at Christmas time and I was surprised when I opened one and it was the Korn CD *Life Is Peachy.* That was because I would look up the lyrics to the songs and would be persistent about how I didn't think they were that bad so my parents finally gave in and let me listen to that type of music. My extra help that I needed in school continued at Trafford Middle with three special needs teachers that I would sometimes go take tests with as well if I needed help or need more time to finish tests.

Just like elementary school, I continued to play in the band. The sixth graders practiced during homeroom and the rest of the band practiced during the afternoon before lunch. Mr. Sam Lebarbra was the same band teacher I had in the Level Green Elementary band. After school, I would go to Monroeville Music Center and take weekly lessons. Every Tuesday I would take my lessons with Bob Abraham, who also had taught my dad how to play the saxophone. My mom and sister also took piano lessons on the same day at the music center. There was one thing I heard about Mr. Abraham before I started taking lessons and that was if you were playing any song with the B-flat note and you missed it, he would yell out, "B-flat". At the end of my sixth-grade year during the summer, before band practice, my family and I drove down to Myrtle Beach, South Carolina, and met up with my aunt, uncle, and my two cousins. One day we were down there and I ran into Mr. Lebarbra at the place where you could rent bicycles and ride them around the beach area. Most of the time was spent at the beach but for part of the trip we drove down to Charlestown and went sightseeing downtown. At first, I didn't want to go but once we got down there I enjoyed it.

During the summer, seventh and eighth graders would have weekly practice. One day at the end of practice, Mr. Lebarbra asked if anyone wanted to stay after practice to join the jazz band. So I ended up joining and really enjoyed it more than the regular band. The reasons that I liked jazz band more were the music was more upbeat and played at a faster pace and also the people that I was in the jazz band with were good at playing the songs. They took the music more seriously and were good at playing it, more so then some of the students during regular band practice that didn't care to learn the songs or just goofed off. Jazz band also got to perform once a year at the Penn Trafford High School for a combined show with both the Trafford and Penn Middle School Jazz Band, which was fun.

At the beginning of my seventh grade year, Damian Sopher, a classmate of mine that also went to Level Green, started attending his first year there. He and I didn't get along during our time at Level Green. He wasn't there in sixth grade and I later found out why. When he first came back, we didn't talk to each other. Halfway through the year, he, Chuck Rainey, and I worked on a project together for our reading class that was wrestling-related. During that time, he and I became friends and any issues we had in the past went away. During my final year at Trafford Middle, I got to play two solos with the jazz band for our Christmas and spring concerts. For the Christmas concert, the song my solo was from was *Charlie Brown Christmas* which was a very difficult solo to play and I somehow managed to play it well. To this day, I'm still surprised that I was able to pull it off and got good responses from my classmates and other people as well. At the spring concert, my solo wasn't nearly as difficult to play as the other one was. The solo was from the song "Night Train Theme". The reason that it was easier was because it wasn't as long and fast-paced as the other one.

Eighth grade was a fun year and very challenging year as well. That year instead of math being my hardest subject, Home economics and reading were very hard for me to do well in. Some of the stories in reading class as well as certain tests dealing with questions from the stories and vocabulary would be very frustrating to figure out. In home economics the big project that year was to sew a design of something, everyone had several choices to pick from. For example, you could sew a teddy bear, a small baseball bat, or a soccer ball. My choice was to sew the soccer ball because it looked the easiest to do of all the other options. Sewing the soccer ball was extremely difficult and several people had to help me out through the process from start to finish. Thankfully, they stayed very patient with me, especially the teacher herself.

Social studies was always my favorite subject in school, especially in both seventh and eighth grade. My seventh grade social studies teacher Mr. John Connolly's class was a lot of fun. Every Friday we got to play a world quiz game with groups of four people and compete against other teams. Each member of a team got to answer a question and if you weren't sure of the answer, Mr. Connolly gave you the option to get help from your teammates and then he would give the correct answer. At one point during the school year, we were learning different capitals of countries. To help us remember the capital of the country Belgium we were told to think of brussel sprouts leading up to our test of naming the capitals. During the test, I put down brussel sprouts as my answer. Afterwards, everyone was sitting there quietly while the teacher was looking at the tests and grading them. Out of nowhere, Mr. Connolly started laughing out loud while he was grading my test and said, "I can't believe you put brussel sprouts as the answer." Instead of taking a point off me, he thought it was funny and gave the point to me. He never forgot that and even signed my eighth grade yearbook, "Tim 'Brussel Sprouts' Cronin, to a great kid that always made me laugh".

Mr. Daily was my eighth grade social studies teacher as well as my homeroom teacher. In his class, we would grab a folder each week with different assignments in it that would be due within a few days of whenever you started it. He was one of those teachers that you could joke around with but be serious whenever he needed to be. Some people asked him if they could do the Eskimo dance and he would always say, "No Eskimo dancing or any other dancing".

Going into the year 2000 on New Year's Eve 1999, there were all types of rumors going around about if the computer systems would crash and not be able to move the transition into the new millennium. My friends and I were thinking that if it happened, school would get canceled. English class that year was your typical English class with spelling tests and the usual grammar lessons minus a couple of things. Number one, if you used the word "like" in a sentence, the teacher had a jar that she would put a marble in each time unless you caught the mistake and told her I said "like". Number two was that every Friday we did an activity called Scope Plays where we would read pages from a movie or an actual play from a magazine. Everyone in the class would be assigned to be different characters from whatever was being read. From time to time someone in class wouldn't pay attention to when it was their turn to read their part and would have to be told several times about it which pissed off the teacher. We also did a weekly journal, which we wrote about different things such as what we did over the weekend, made-up word abbreviations using the letters of our first name, and, at the very beginning of the school year, list three goals we wanted to achieve by the end of the year. One of my goals was to study for tests at least two to three days in advance which I did and was proud of the fact that goal was able to be accomplished.

In the spring of 2000 at a karate tournament, I competed in both sparring and forms competitions. For the forms competition, I didn't place within the top three places. However in sparring, I ended up placing second. Shortly after the tournament, I took my black belt test and passed. Leading up to that day, I kept telling my dad, "Someday I'm going to be a black belt." Towards the end of the year, all the eighth graders gathered in the auditorium and listened to some students from Penn Trafford High School talk about what to expect going to school there. It didn't last long and based on what was said I couldn't wait till I started going there.

Unfortunately, an incident happened at the end of the school year involving another student. The culprit vandalized my yearbook along with some other student's books, the student not only got ISS (In School Suspension) but had to pay for new yearbooks as well. The only problem was that with getting a new yearbook was getting the same signatures twice from certain people. Whenever I approached those people, they would remember signing the first time and told me, "I already signed this". I explained the situation to them and they understood and had no problem with it. However, there were some people that hadn't signed the first one I got. My friend Chuck Rainey told our reading teacher that I had to get a second yearbook and after that, she made an announcement to the class about what happened. Chuck was the very first person to sign it and wrote, "Dear Tim, to your new yearbook, Chuck." Following Chuck, a few of the other students came up after him and wrote things as well. That was a very kind gesture on his part to do that for me. Even though he didn't have to, it really meant a lot to me. There was a tradition on the last day of school whenever the eighth graders were leaving on the bus. The eighth grade teachers stood outside and waved goodbye to all those students. Only four more years of school left to go.

PART 3

HIGH SCHOOL

There were things that I heard about freshmen being given a tough time by other students, especially the upper classmen. To my surprise that really wasn't the case. That summer during band practice and band camp, I met a lot of nice people ranging from all the freshmen to the sophomores, juniors, and seniors. Band practice was held every Tuesday night for three hours. During those three hours, we practiced the music we would perform for the Friday night football games and Saturday night band competitions. Learning the forward and backward marching techniques was the first thing each section did. Marching backwards was easier for me to pick up on opposed to forward marching. Mr. Green told me one night during practice, "You're doing better with your backward marching then with your forward marching." I did have problems with my two section leaders and the band instructor Mr. Monteleone. Each section had section leaders that consisted of upper classmen, one senior and one junior. Diana was the senior, and Bob was the junior, both could be nasty at times.

During band camp the one day, at sectionals, the sectionals teacher had us do this thing called Spotlight Theatre. He asked everyone in the alto saxophone section to play the opening song of our show. We were asked to turn our music stands around and play the song from memory. If you didn't know the song, you could say, "I only know part of the song, may I use the music sheet?" Then you could. Most of the section could play it from memorization and some couldn't. There were two people in the section that didn't know the song and felt the wrath of both section leaders. Both people in the section had to do pushups and the one individual got yelled at by both section leaders as well. The senior section leader yelled at the one guy that didn't know the song and said, "Dave, you are a junior," while the junior section leader said to him, "You're making us look bad." In my opinion both Diana and Bob were both out of line by the way they were going off on Dave. I understood their frustration because the section leaders would be the ones to take the fall, however I feel there was a better way to handle the situation. During the month of August, we had band camp and would get a drill sheet with an assigned number, marking where our position was on the field during the show. The first week of camp, we were at the high school from 8 AM to 12 PM. After that it was from 8 AM to 4 PM.

During band camp the one day, Mr. Monteleone out of nowhere yelled out at freshmen Mike S. who was in the tenor saxophone section. "Mike, is that how we march with our instrument in our ear? Mike, why don't you come up here and show the entire band how you were marching?" For some reason, the band director didn't like some of the freshmen that year. Mike went up in front of the entire band. When everyone saw how he was marching, everyone in the band laughed at him. There was absolutely no need to single him out in front of everyone. A trumpet player Matt C. was sitting on the field during break time and Mr. M yelled at him, "Until you can march this show perfect, then you can sit down ninth grader." Prior to that, I'd never dealt with any teacher like this guy that did things such as that to students.

After band camp was finished, our first performance was our preview show at the end of August. Following the show, there was the preview show dance in the school cafeteria with a DJ and people dancing, which was a wonderful way to relax and have fun. To end the summer, we performed along with other high school bands at Kennywood in the Fall Fantasy Parade and afterwards we got to stay on the park for a little bit before getting back on the bus to head back to the school. That Monday was the first day of my freshmen year, before that I had gotten my schedule of classes at freshmen orientation so I walked around the school to see where my homeroom was and where my different classrooms were located. My math teacher was at the school that night and he introduced himself and said, "I'm Mr. Simpson, your math teacher." That was a great idea, because that very first day I had no problems finding where I needed to go while most of the freshmen asked around. The only problem that I encountered was finding where my locker was at, after that day it was a breeze.

Every Tuesday night band practice was held. One night, we were doing marching exercises, I heard my name being called over the speakers, "Tim Cronin, roll your feet and turn your shoulders. You see ladies and gentlemen, I'm singling out individuals." To make things worse my section leader, Diana, kept yelling at me, "Tim, you're not there". She was referring to the fact that I wasn't in the correct position on the field.

That night really pissed me off, I was trying my best with everything and it wasn't easy for me to catch on with some of those things, apparently it wasn't good enough for either individual that night. Because of that, I would vent to my parents and friends about my problems in band, especially with the senior section leader. My dad and some other people from band told me not to worry about it, that she's a senior and I wouldn't have to deal with her after the end of the year. At the end of every Friday night football game, the entire band walked over to the Penn Trafford student section and played our Alma Mater regardless of whether the team won or lost. It was fun to perform at halftime and we went to all the games both home and away. That year Penn Trafford made it to the playoffs and the first playoff game was a home game where we hosted North Allegheny High School. Penn Trafford lost that night and that was the end of marching season and the start of the concert season.

During the first half of concert season, everyone practiced together for our Christmas Concert. After that, the tenth, eleventh and twelfth graders had practice during fifth period, while the ninth graders practiced during eighth period. One thing everyone had to do was record a cassette tape with a song that was picked by our band instructor and was assigned a number such as "Alto-Saxophone #9", "Trumpet #5", and "Clarinet #7". The percussion section stayed after school and did their auditions in the band room. After a few days, Mr. Monteleone would read everyone's score out loud and the number chair you got depended on how well you scored. The highest number got first chair and the lowest score got last chair. My freshmen, sophomore, and Junior year, I got second chair, which was great. There was one stipulation to the tapes, the recorded tape could only be of the song you had to play and if there was any type of background noise in it you got an F grade. At the spring concert, the freshmen performed their songs first and then after that the rest of the band played their songs. Towards the end of the concert, all the seniors had their names announced one at a time followed by where they were going to attend college and what they were going to major in. To wrap up the concert the freshmen joined the rest of the band and played the song, "Stars and Stripes Forever".

After the school year was over, I went on my first band trip to Disneyworld in June 2001 which was a lot of fun. We had rehearsals in the morning before heading to one of the Disney parks each day. We got to explore the parks on our own minus the times we had to report to our assigned chaperones. One night we were going to see the Fantasia show at MGM Studios, minutes before the show was supposed to start, out of nowhere, it began to thunder and pour down rain. No one in the band had umbrellas or ponchos, therefore everyone took off running toward the busses which didn't help because we all got soaking wet. One of the last nights we were at Disney, we performed in the parade at night which was a blast, in my opinion, compared to performing at the football games. Whenever we were done performing at the away football games, band competitions, and at Disney, our band trailer came with us and there was a procedure that everyone had to follow. The percussion section went into the trailer first and put their things away, then the rest of the band got to go in after that. Some people after the parade broke procedure and after everyone was done putting their instruments away, we got yelled at by our instructor for breaking procedure, which wasn't the only time that happened.

One Tuesday night during band practice heading into my sophomore year the drum major Nick noticed my forward marching was improving and told me, "excellent job". During band camp one day, a bunch of us were sitting around in the band room during break time when Nick told us, "Get out, the new principal is coming." One person was making a getaway for the exit door when the principal, Mr. Inglese, saw the individual and told him to get back inside. What happened next I'll never forget. The first words that he said were, "It is not the custodian's job to clean this place." Everyone in the room all looked at each other in shock and confusion. Unfortunately, it didn't end there either. We went back on the field and had to stand at attention while the principal told Mr. M what happened and were standing at attention for about five to ten minutes. From what I understand, someone scratched up part of the floor with a soda can. After a few minutes, one of the seniors, Jon M., confessed to doing it. I don't think Jon was the culprit, he just wanted to move on with practice so that we wouldn't have to keep standing there. Practice kept going on and we proceeded to do our pre-football song and formation that we did for our home games.

Tuesday, September 11th, 2001, as has been said multiple times, is a day that America will never forget. I was in my computer class that morning when an announcement was made over the intercom. All that was said was, "There's nothing we can do about this tragedy, we're safe where we are." The T.V. wasn't on in the classroom and therefore nobody knew what the announcement was about. Later that day during fifth period for band practice, I asked my classmate Brian Witt what was going on. He told me that terrorists hijacked airplanes and crashed them into the World Trade Center in New York City. I was very shocked like everyone else was and didn't know how to react. When I got home my Mom had the T.V. on and saw not only the World Trade Center but also the Pentagon had been attacked. Later I found out about the brave passengers of Flight 93 that fought back against the terrorists and prevented them from crashing the airplane into the White House and instead crashed it into the ground in Somerset county. First responders as well as the passengers on Flight 93 were the real heroes on that horrific day.

The next day, President George W. Bush asked that all schools held an assembly and all the students gathered in the gym to sing, "God Bless America". Penn Trafford ended up canceling the football game that Friday night which ended up being played Saturday afternoon. On top of that, the band also had a band competition that same day in the evening which ended up being the only time in my four years of band that we ended up pulling double duty. We didn't score that high in the competition because it was a long day and some people didn't care about their performances on the field. One of the frustrating things about being in the band was that you had people that didn't care about learning the music or how their deficient performance affected things.

The summer of 2002 was a fun one for me. In June at the Mellon Arena, my friend Damian Sopher and I went to see the band Korn in concert, which was my very first concert. Most of that summer was spent at Vo-Tech which was a trade school a lot of students attended during the school year. There were a few things that you could go for such as automotive and graphic arts, which was the one I ended up doing and I didn't want to attend. After a few days it was fun and was glad that was a big part of my summer. It also helped that my friend DJ Ashbaugh who went to High School with me was in the graphic arts program to show me the ropes. There was one day that I didn't attend because the church that I attended was taking a trip to Cedar Point. That was the first time I visited there and really enjoyed the park. It had a lot of coasters, more then any other amusement park. The day we went was on the day before my eighteenth birthday, which was great because it was a pre-birthday celebration.

Instead of the school year starting on the last Monday in August as it did in the past, my junior year started the Thursday before. Junior year was a momentous year for certain reasons. The teacher that I had for social studies, Mr. Crovak told us that our homework assignments weren't due until the day of our tests and the science class that I took, Earth and Space Science, was a lot of fun to learn. About 95% of my science class were seniors and the only juniors were Ryan Skuta, Kate Campbell, and I. At first, I didn't know this until a few days into class, some of the seniors were cheerleaders and a couple of them were nice to me, Nikki Braun and Kristin Merolla. One week we were in the planetarium learning about the different constellations in the sky and what they looked like. There was one day we were in the planetarium

22

with my former sophomore science teacher Mr Sullivan, who was now the assistant vice–principal, sat in during class. A bunch of students were talking during class which got the rest of the class chewed out the next day. Ms. Forys told us, "You guys know better than to talk during class, especially when the vice-principal is here." Our punishment was that the whole class had to answer a bunch of questions from a chapter in the science book we had. That was the third time that happened to a class that I was in for punishment, twice in sixth grade and that day. Around Christmas time, the high school jazz band along with Encore from the chorus department went and performed at the elementary schools. I really enjoyed jazz band in middle school and my sophomore year I ended up joining the high school jazz band. The students in Encore would go up to the microphone on stage, introduce themselves, and say their name followed by, "I would like to say 'Hi' to all my former teachers".

At the beginning of 2003, I joined a teen support group for people that had a form of autism. That's where I met my friends Joel Brewton, Doug Biel, Dale Johnston, Matt Jamison, Chris Gamrat, and Matt Carroll. Craig Academy in Pittsburgh, PA was where we had our weekly sessions on Thursday nights. Julie was our therapist that we had for a few months before she ended up going back to school to get her master's degree. After that, Mike took her place. During sessions, we videotaped role-playing involving different social scenarios. One scenario involved Doug and I playing characters under different names. In the scenario, Doug's character was talking to me while my character was supposed to me looking back and forth at my watch while Doug was talking to me. Instead, I just looked down at my watch. After a minute, Mike said "cut" and started laughing. He told me, "You're supposed to look down at your watch and then look back up. Don't just stare at it the entire time." Another thing we learned was how to interact with women, such as how to ask them out on a date. It also said if the date involved going to see a movie and the woman wanted to see a romantic movie and you wanted to see the new Star Wars movie, the thing to do was to see the romantic movie. Once a week, I would have one-on-one sessions with Mike to talk about whatever I wanted to talk with him about.

The band spring trip in April 2003 was supposed to be at Busch Gardens in Williamsburg, Virginia. I was looking forward to going because when my older sister was in the high school band, she went her junior year. We found out at the end of the 2001-02 school year that the trip was going to be at Disney again. For some reason Mr. M really loved Disney World. That year we didn't go after school was out for the year which was nice since Disney wasn't as crowded as in the spring time. The only problem was that there was an obstacle of picking what day to leave. Easter Sunday was going to be the original planned day to leave out and there was a bunch of objections from the band parents about leaving that day. The school board was the reason that we couldn't go to Disney in the summer, mainly because of the seniors. Their diplomas would've had to been withheld until they returned from the trip. Plus, the biggest factor was they wouldn't have been part of the school anymore. If anything would've happened to them, the school wouldn't have been able to do anything. The class of 2003 had some trouble makers and wouldn't have been able to be punished by the school.

It wasn't as warm when we went the second time around which was a huge plus and the lines for rides weren't too long. I hung out with the same group of people for the most part and during that trip I started talking to and hanging out with some people that I hadn't really interacted with before. One of the days of the trip was when we got to go to Blizzard Beach, their water park, and a wonderful way to cool off from the heat. The band members had the option to go to

Blizzard Beach or just go to MGM Studios. Most of the band went to Blizzard Beach. Their Lazy River was unlike any other one that I'd experienced before. There was a giant house off to the right with an open chimney that had the "a-choo" sneeze effect and when it sneezed water came shooting out of the top. Me and a bunch of band members were on the Lazy River at the same time. It was as if our own takeover of the ride was happening. The Fantasia show that we tried to see the previous band trip turned out great this time. We got to see the show without any severe weather interruptions and the show itself was great. A couple of days later we packed up our things and got on the buses to head back home.

While most everyone didn't look forward to leaving, I wanted to end the school year so that finally my senior year could begin. I looked forward to not only graduating, but also to make the most out of my last year at school. At the end of my junior year, Mr. M signed my yearbook telling me, "I think you've come a long way, Tim, looking forward to next year". That was great that he wrote that. Part of my senior year didn't go as well as I hoped it would, making good memories was what I was hoping to accomplish and did for the most part.

There was a work program that I signed up for. Goodwill was the place that I was supposed to be working at for a few hours during the school day and would come back at the end of the day. That year there was a considerable number of freshmen coming to the high school that caused some changes to be made. Because of that, the work program didn't happen. With that happening, my entire schedule had to be redone. My dad signed me up for two math classes instead of one, which led to an argument with me getting mad at him and asking why he did that. His reason was to help me improve my math skills. My counter-argument was that my dad knew how stressful math was for me and I didn't like the idea. The two math courses were Business

Math and Cognitive Tutor Geometry. Business Math was easier for me to understand then Geometry. However, parts of Business Math were still difficult. For the third year in a row, I took a computer class and struggled with this course more than the previous two. All three were hard for me to follow for some reason.

The biggest problem of my senior year was getting harassed by two other seniors in my class, Brendan C. and Mike S. Despite me asking them nicely to stop several times, they couldn't take the hint, especially Mike. Brendan wasn't as nasty as Mike was but my problem with Brendan is that, from time to time, he initiated the harassment and Mike went along with it. Before this, Mike and I were friends. We talked and hung out for most of the band trip to Disney our junior year. His change in behavior towards me in our senior year caught me off-guard. He said and did some horrible things to me. We were getting ready for our final jazz band performance at our Spring Concert. A few of us were hanging around, talking in the room we practiced in when Mike pulled a dog bone out of his pocket, threw it, and told me to go fetch it. That made me angry and I walked out of the room. What kind of an eighteen-year-old high school senior does that? To add insult to injury, the one day he had the nerve to call me a loser and told me that I wouldn't amount to be anything. My friend Steve Whiteman, another senior, noticed what was going on and stuck up for me. He even saw Brendan and Mike mocking something that I was doing and told them, "The kid isn't dumb. He knows what you're doing."

Now I'll talk about the positives of my senior year. Getting to enjoy all the friends in band I had that wouldn't see much of after the end of the year and having my last performances with them at band shows and football games. I especially enjoyed graduation rehearsals and not having to show up on the last day of school until everyone else was gone, the band banquet, and last but certainly not least, my senior band trip to New York City. Towards the end of marching season at a home football game was Senior Night. The parents of the seniors would be on the sideline prior to the start of the game and the announcer would call the students name and say, "son or daughter of…" followed by the parents' names. Before the game, the seniors would get gifts from the rest of the members in their section and after the game we got to have what was called the Senior Tea, where all the seniors and parents got to have snacks and drinks. A few weeks later, I performed for the very last time in the marching competition show PIMBA, which was the big championship competition for all the high school bands. Just to name a few, there was Gateway, Woodland Hills, Kiski, and other bands from the different Quad Sections, Class A, AA, AAA, and Quad A, which Penn Trafford and Gateway were in. That night for the very first time after we got our trophy, we got to meet Jack, who designed the drill sheet and formations that we used for our show. He talked to us for a few minutes and told us how well we performed. It was a great moment to finally meet Jack and hear what he had to say.

During our visit to Trafford Middle School for our Jazz Band Christmas concert, I got to visit four of my former teachers for a little bit before we had to get ready for our show. Some of us walked into Mr. Daily's classroom and when he saw me walking in he said, "oh no, not this guy". He of course was joking around. One thing all the seniors had to do before they graduated English Class was to do a research paper on whatever subject they wanted. That was the case with my English teacher Mr. Bechtell, who called me "Croney". There was another English Teacher, Ms. Kelley, and my friend from band, Matt Calfe, told me in Ms. Kelley's class their research paper had to be about what they wanted to do after high school. For my research paper, I chose to do it on World War II. The reason for choosing that subject was that my two grandfathers served in the war.

Not only did you have to type up a paper, but you also had to present a version of your paper using Windows Media for a slide show presentation. Mr. Bechtell asked who wanted to present first, second, third, and so on. I ended up being the sixth person to present. Some people were nervous about getting up and speaking in front of the class, which is understandable for certain people. Throughout my school years that was never an issue for me, and I presented with no problems at all. My teacher couldn't believe it and told me, "You weren't nervous at all." My classmates told me how great a job I did. The reason that I decided to be number six was to that I could get it out of the way because going last wasn't what I liked to do.

Before finals, all the seniors in the band went on a trip to New York City. We left on Friday, May 14th, 2004 and got back on Sunday night, May 16th. Friday night, we arrived late because there were problems with the bus and left an hour later then we should've. Saturday we got to visit the Empire State Building and went up to the observation deck at the very top, which had a magnificent view of the city. That afternoon, we got to take a boat ride over to Ellis Island. Before boarding the boat, everyone had to go through metal detectors.

After I went through a security woman called me over while I was gathering up my items and said, "Sir, can you please step over here?" So I did. In front of me was this machine where someone stepped into it, put their hands on top of their head, and held that position for a few seconds. After doing that and boarding the boat, I asked Matt Calfe what that machine was. He told me the machine was used to scan someone's body to detect if they had drugs on them. There must've been something about me that caused them to randomly pick me out of the crowd.

On the boat ride over to Ellis Island, we got to see the Statue of Liberty. However, we were told that it was still closed off to tourists due to the city wanting to prevent a terrorist attack. We got over to the island and got to walk around to check it out. Some of my Ancestors came over from Ireland to America so I got to see their names written on plaques, which was great to see. That evening was the best part of the entire trip. We walked around Times Square, ate at one of the restaurants for dinner, and went into the Toys R Us which had a Ferris wheel inside of it. To top off the evening, we got to see the Lion King on Broadway. The seats we were in were up top where part of the orchestra played. If you're in New York City and get the chance to see Lion King on Broadway, I would highly recommend it. The show was a wonderful experience. After the show was over, we went outside and it was pouring down rain. Déjà vu all over again just like our freshmen Disney trip. Most of the students made a run for the bus while a bunch of us took shelter underneath the roof of a building, some had umbrellas. While we were waiting for the rain to die down, limo after limo was driving by. Mr. M joked around and said, "Let's jump inside." He then asked me, "Tim, do you remember when this happened at Disney?"

The last day we were there, people split up into various groups with a chaperone and explored different areas of the city. Sunday afternoon we ate lunch in Grand Central Station where we ate pizza at one of the many food places inside followed by going into Trump Tower. The lower level was as far as we could go which was fine because I could say that I got to visit the tower. Our trip ended with that and we got back on the bus to go back home. Again we got back late again and had to get up early for school the next morning. That morning, I overslept and almost missed the bus. My mom drove me to the bus stop, and I got to catch the bus right as it was leaving. The teachers couldn't believe how tired we were. Matt Calfe said it best, "You try walking around New York City for two days and see how tired you are."

Next up was the band banquet that was held every year on the Friday night before Memorial Day weekend. There were awards given out with distinct categories. One award was given out under the category "The Section That Couldn't March". Of course the alto saxophone section won that award. Brian Witt presented the award to Brandon and Nicole, the two juniors in our section and told them, "It's your section now." All the seniors got gym bags and a plaque with their picture on it taken during the previous summer. After dinner we watched a video with pictures and video highlights from the 2003-2004 year which ended with the seniors coming out one at a time waving goodbye or doing something else. The banquet always ended with dancing and I got to dance with two friends, Jessie Foutz and Emily Phillips. "Piano Man" was the last song played that night. Steve, Matt, Shawnee, me, and a few others danced in a circle to end the night of our final banquet. Finally came the graduation rehearsals and the big day we all waited for, graduation. While I was walking up to get my diploma, a bunch of the band members yelled my name. High School was finally over and I was filled with joy and excitement.

Construction Tour of West Coast Racers at Six Flags Magic Mountain during CoasterCon 42.

Joel Brewton, Ken Riling (Middle),
and I getting a selfie at the Santa Monica Pier.

Getting a post Wedding photo taken with my Parents, My Cousins,
Katie and Austin as well as my Aunt Terina, my Cousin Dylan and his
Wife, Lauren.

CoasterCon 41 Banquet Attire.

My good friend Mark and I getting a picture taken with Hillia Hula at Belmont Park on the Boardwalk near Mission Beach.

Pre-Spring Con 2018 Dinner at Lamberts Café.

PART 4

MOVING FORWARD

The summer of 2004 was a very memorable and fun one for me. On June 19, my sister Andrea got married to her fiancé Zach Washa. They had a big turn-out for their big day with mainly relatives from both sides of the families. Zach asked me to be in the wedding party, so I said yes. After the wedding, the bride and groom got their pictures taken at Phipps Conservatory in Pittsburgh followed by the reception in Wilmerding.

In April, Joel Brewton told me about this Roller Coaster Club called ACE (American Coaster Enthusiasts) which I never heard of before. He told me that the club was going to Cedar Point for their June event CoasterCon and asked if I wanted to go. Since I enjoyed Cedar Point the first time that I went, I said I would go back. May 19 was the day that I officially became a member of ACE. CoasterCon is ACE's big national event that's held every June for a week. The week-long event includes morning ERT before the public gets into the park and evening ERT after the park is closed for the day, breakfast and other meals, prizes, and the annual banquet that's held either a few days into con or at the end of it. I left the day after the wedding that Sunday afternoon and arrived that evening. Attending my first ACE Event, I didn't know what to expect. CoasterCon exceeded my expectations with the overall experience that both Cedar Point (the host park) and Geauga Lake, the other park did for ACE. It was a lot of fun.

Also that summer, I attended some graduation parties, including holding one of my own in July, then went to one the week after for my friend, Amanda Thomas. The day after her graduation party, my brother-in-law Zach and I went to a wrestling show at the Mellon Arena, specifically WWE Monday Night Raw. As I mentioned before, during my childhood I didn't enjoy going to the shows. We went to four Raw shows and I enjoyed them. Eventually, my dad and I went to many shows after that. He could tell I enjoyed them more than I used to.

It felt strange not going to weekly band practice on Tuesday nights and not getting up early for band camp every morning. There were a few times I got to see my friends from band. They were happy to see me and I was happy to see and talk to them. Leading up to the end of summer, I wasn't sure what I wanted to major in at CCAC. My dad found this course in the CCAC catalog entitled Central Sterile Processing. After reading the description of the course, it didn't sound that bad to me. Parts of it weren't easy, but for the first half of the year it wasn't hard to understand the material.

While I was attending school, my first job was at Bob Evans in Monroeville as a bus boy that cleaned tables after people were done eating at them. It was their busiest time of the year whenever I started. When winter time rolled around, things slowed down then picked up again when the weather started to warm up. The bosses I had were friendly for the most part except for one, Dave, who was nasty. The first time that I saw him was when this other bus boy Frank and I were cleaning dishes in the kitchen. Frank told Dave, "Hey Dave, I've been here almost five years now, how about a raise?"

Dave got angry and yelled "No". When he tried walking away, Frank yelled, "Yes!" The conservation ended with Dave coming back in and yelling, "No" again. He got real snippy with me a few times. I'm not sure why he did. Some people couldn't handle the workplace at Bob Evans and ended up walking out on the job.

Back to CCAC, the first half of Central Sterile Processing involved the distribution aspect of things, such as how high off the ground you could store things and how high they could be stored from the ceiling. FIFO (First In, First Out) was an acronym that was used for rotating stock items on each shelf, using items that had a shorter expiration date then others. Learning the different instruments was the second half of the course, identifying different instruments such as retractors, forceps, and other specialty items. Part of the course also included going to a hospital and learning the job hands-on by assembling different trays with instruments we learned and how to clean them as well.

One thing that I struggled with was wrapping. Whether it was a basin or loaner tray, the technique of it always got me and the supervisor, Carol, got frustrated after a while with showing me how. Other than that, the rest of the job I caught onto quickly. The clinical lasted a few months, then after was my graduation from CCAC in which I received a certificate in Sterile Processing.

Allegheny General Hospital was the place where my clinical took place originally, but my preferred choice was at Forbes Regional in Monroeville since that was the closest place to me. Linda Radsvin, who oversaw the clinicals, informed me that Forbes wasn't doing clinicals at that time. Following graduation, I started putting in job applications at four different hospitals, Allegheny General, Mercy Jeanette, Mercy Hospital in Downtown Pittsburgh, and Westmoreland Hospital in Greensburg. The only interviews that I got were at the two Mercy locations. The one in Jeanette was a 3 PM to 11:30 PM full-time position. Unfortunately at the time that shift didn't work out because I wasn't driving and the Westmoreland bus didn't run that often. Two weeks later was my interview at the other Mercy Hospital with the supervisor Randy Swartz. During the interview, Randy pulled out different instruments out of a tray and I had to name them all, thankfully it was just basic instrumentation. There were only a couple of instruments that I couldn't name correctly and other than that the interview went well. At the time, the position was only part-time with the potential to go full-time. There were several shifts in the department. Along with SPS staff being split up, five people worked downstairs, two on daylight and three on evenings. Upstairs in the center of the OR was the OR workroom which had more SPS Staff than downstairs. While I was in training, the first four weeks of the job were spent on the daylight shifts, two on 6 AM to 2:30 PM and the last two on 7 AM to 3:30 PM. After that was done, I started on 11 AM to 7:30 PM which became my steady shift.

Downstairs the job duties included cleaning and assembling trays from same-day surgery, clinics, and the OR (which only included open-heart and aneurysm), going to the different floors to pick up and clean pumps, commodes, and other items, and last but not least we had to clean and restock crash carts as well as put away stock that was ordered from distribution. Upstairs I just cleaned and assembled all the cases from OR and wrapped loaner trays that came in from an outside vendor company.

Things didn't start out that well for me at Mercy. For some reason it was difficult for me to learn the job, mainly with pickup, while my problems with wrapping continued. Randy was hard on me, being frustrated about my struggles with wrapping items. One day she yelled at me and said, "Unacceptable, was that acceptable at AGH?" To me, that was unprofessional for a supervisor to go off on someone like that.

It turns out that I wasn't the only employee she treated badly. As a result, Human Resources punished her. After a while, Randy and I got along much better and she even told me how much I was improving.

My fifth week on the job, I met the other two guys that worked evenings, Glenn Foy and Sideek Vick. Sideek worked 12 PM to 8:30 PM and Glenn was from 3 PM to 11:30 PM. I'll never forget the very first day I met Glenn. Leading up to the day I met him, one of the things that my coworkers told me was that he yelled. The yelling wasn't what I thought it was, the yelling was just him talking loudly. Anyway, there I was working on a tray when, out of nowhere, he walks up to me and says, "You must be the new guy. Hi, I'm Glenn." Him talking loudly at first threw me off guard and I didn't know how to respond. There was silence on my end for a few seconds but finally my response was, "Hi I'm Tim."

Pickup was one of my main job duties for my shift. There was a sheet you had to fill out with your name and date on it. Also, there was the list of items with a blank space next to it, marking how many of each item were picked up from the floors. There were seven different floors we had to pick up from. Items on the sheet got marked off such as five pumps, three commodes, and three wall suctions. Upon completion, the next step was to take the dirty items to the back and clean them in our decontamination area. Everything for the most part got wiped down by hand, minus the commodes that got cleaned inside our cart washer which was also used to clean our dirty case carts. Assembling trays wasn't that hard, all you had to do was follow a count sheet with the instrument name and other specialty items as well such as Weitlaner retractor, adson forceps with and without teeth, deaver, malleable, and, if you assembled an open-heart tray, cooley retractor, and tuffier. Our count sheets were laminated compared to other hospitals where the count sheets were marked off with your name and date the tray was done on.

Occasionally, we would get a phone call to put up a traction set up in a patient's room. The traction set up consisted of several bars that were connected and was put on the outside of the patient's bed. Whenever the patient was discharged from the hospital, we would get a call to come pick up the pieces that were taken down by one of the nurses on the floor. Every week stock was ordered by Annabelle who worked daylight and was in charge whenever Randy was off. There were several racks of items that needed to be restocked, some items were used less than other items were. Suture needles were used more often because there were specialty trays used by the different clinics and the extra items that needed to be put with them were listed on the count sheet. For all the trays assembled either from same day surgery or the OR, everyone downstairs had a numbered code that they put in the computer along with the tray or item that was going to be sterilized. The next step after that was to stamp the item with a load sticker consisting of the sterilizer number, the date the load was run, and the load number.

The two types of sterilization used that were used were steam and gas. Three was the number that we had for both methods of sterilization. For the gas, it had a number four, five, and eight. Number four was the big machine that was used the most, mainly because of the size of the load being run. The other two were small sterilizers and would be run later in the evening. There were a lot of gas items that had to be done so we always ran two loads a day. Gas sterilization took longer to complete a load due to the fact of aeration being a twelve-hour cycle. Therefore, the two loads had to be run early. Steam cycles took an hour to run a load and after that was done, the door got cranked open to let the load sit in the autoclave for an additional forty-five minutes before it could get taken out.

The first thing that was done after the load was sterilized was to record the biological in a book we had with the lot number along with the date and time the bio was put in the bio-reader. Biologicals would be read for both steam and gas after three hours. The way it would be read was by a minus symbol. If a load had a positive biological read out, the load would have to be redone completely. The reason being was that meant there were micro-organisms or bacteria, therefore the load wasn't sterile. It was a rare occurrence for that to happen.

After the readout was done, confirming the biological tested negative, and the sterile items were cooled down, everything was put on a clean case cart, covered up, and taken to the departments. Mistakes were made with either OR items going to SDS or to Labor and Delivery, SDS going to OR, and vice versa. It happened so much to the point that eventually Randy made us not only sign a sheet with our names on it, but also made us put a card with where the cart was going. The card idea really helped, which helped to eliminate the number of errors being made. Things got better as time went on with being able to do everything and thought the crew I worked with was a lot of fun.

At the end of 2007, everyone that worked at Mercy was informed by the person that oversaw the hospital that it was going to be bought by UPMC. Prior to that announcement, employees went into panic mode starting rumors that Mercy was closing and thought they would lose their jobs. Apparently, there was another buyer that was interested in buying which was Allegheny Health Network. AHN didn't have the money to buy out Mercy that UPMC did. Other than the name of the hospital changing, there wasn't anything affected. Instead of being able to clock in seven minutes before our start time and seven minutes prior to leaving, with UPMC it went down to five minutes for both. Additionally, there was a new doctor in the OR which added to us downstairs cleaning and sterilizing some additional items on top of what we were already reprocessing. The one tray had to soak in the sink with enzymatic for a while because of the fact there were items in the tray that needed to be flushed out with a syringe because they were bloody.

Towards the beginning of the summer of 2008, the Department of Veterans Affairs was hiring for sterile processing. Mike M., who was one of the staff that worked upstairs in the OR workroom at Mercy, applied for a job there and started working at the VA in January 2008. My friend Tamika Scales and I also applied for the job and both of us got hired. Before my start date, I had to pass a physical and attend orientation for three days. Shortly after completing the application, Randy got a call from Human Resources at the VA, calling to ask some questions about me. On the day they called, I was off on vacation. When my vacation was done, the first thing upon coming back, Randy called me into her office. She told me the VA called and was happy for me, knowing that I would be making more money, yet heard about the supervisor and were a little concerned about me. After passing the physical and having a successful background check, it was onto the next step.

A few days prior to leaving Mercy, Randy talked to me and told me it was hard for me at first, but after a while I caught onto things and she was real proud of me. Tamika, Glenn, and I went to Dave and Busters to celebrate our hiring at the VA. It was a great night and we ended up staying for a while. For my last day at Mercy, my coworker's downstairs brought in a cake. After we were done eating, the staff on the daylight shift wished me good luck. At the end of my shift, Glenn and Sideek also said the same thing. After that, Glenn got a small cart and wheeled the cake downstairs to where my dad was waiting for me to pick me up. Following my departure from Mercy, I had a few days off before starting orientation at the VA.

Mayhem Festival was the name of a concert out in Burgettstown, outside of Pittsburgh, which was a concert involving all heavy metal bands. My dad didn't want me to go by myself and ended up coming with me, despite my warnings of what it was going to be like. There were some bands that I never heard of before such as Walls of Jericho and Five Finger Death Punch. I It was great to see them perform, especially with Walls of Jericho having a woman singer. The headlining bands were Disturbed and Slipknot. I was a huge fan of both bands and Slipknot had an awesome performance. On my other days off, I met my friend Dale at Sandcastle. My last day, I went to see the new X-Files movie.

That Monday was the first day of orientation in which everyone sat in a small classroom and was given a brief lecture about how things were run at the VA. Next up was a discussion about all the benefits we had the option to choose from. The next two days we spent in the auditorium, which included a video about protecting your information on the computer and the dress code as well. Towards the end of the second day, everyone was asked to stand up say their name and what their job title was. August 3, 2008 was my official start date, which fell on a Sunday, with August 7, 2008 being my very first day on the job. The first thing I did was meet the supervisor, Denise T., who had me fill out a bunch of paperwork in her office and gave me a notebook to fill out what I did in the workroom. Denise then took me into the workroom, introduced me to the rest of the staff, and then put me on tray assembly the rest of the day. For the first three weeks that's what my job assignment was.

After the first couple of weeks, I was anxious to get trained on the other duties. The three duties were case carts, decontamination, and sterilization, with case carts only being done by the daylight shift. At the time I started, everyone rotated through five different shifts, 6 AM to 2:30 PM, 7 AM to 3:30 PM, 10:30 AM to 7 PM, 11:30 AM to 8 PM, and 1 PM to 9:30 PM. There was a lead tech hired for the 1 to

9:30 shift and the woman who got the position was the former evening supervisor at Mercy Hospital in the OR Workroom, Barb, who had that exact same shift.

Case carts were the next job duty I got trained on. My coworker, Lynette, showed me the ropes on what to do. The duties included making up different case carts based on what surgery it was for on the OR case schedule, such as a laparoscopic, open-heart, vascular, thoracic, and so on for the next day's cases. Every Monday and Thursday morning you had to put in a solution order with a list of items that were needed to be stocked in the cast cart area such as sterile water, 1,000 ML normal saline bottles, 3,000 ML normal saline bags, and other assorted items. Besides doing our own solution order, Corney, the OR Anes tech, would call down every morning for a solution order of what was needed upstairs. One of the OR techs or nurses would also call the case cart person for a stock order which was different from the solution order. It wasn't everyday a stock order was needed, some days they didn't call for one, while other days there was a big order of supplies needed. Towards the end of the day, the next day's carts needed for first cases were sent up along with the stock order. After that was done, the person on case carts stocked different packs from the hallway that were used to make up carts. The last thing to do was make up five to six general carts. Mid-shifts and evening shifts rotated between tray assembly, decontamination, and sterilization.

After my week on case carts was done, my next training was in decontamination on the 1 to 9:30 shift. Working in evenings in Decontam involved more items that needed to be cleaned as opposed to the daylight shift, though there were some days that daylight would be busier than usual. Whenever a case was finished, the OR would call down and give the number of dirty carts that needed to be picked up. We would go upstairs, get the carts, take them downstairs, and clean the items inside the cart. During the morning, distribution went upstairs to the different floors to collect pumps, commodes, and other items that were cleaned in Decontam every morning. The Heinz VA and Highland Drive VA would send over their items from their dental clinics. Highland Dental would be dropped off in the morning and Heinz in the afternoon. Heinz VA also had a distribution department that would send over dirty pumps along with other things in a separate cart once a week. Twice in the same month I was trained in Decontam on evening shift. Honestly, it wasn't that hard to learn, aside from putting some instrumentation through the window instead of the washer because of how delicate they were.

My final training process was sterilization that had a lot more detail involved than the previous place I was at. We weren't allowed to stamp anything on the loads before they went in and had to document them twice, once before the load went into the sterilizer and the second time was after the sterile load was finished. After the load was finished, we had to write the items that were run in two different notebooks, one for the OR and the other for the clinics. Event-related was the way most hospitals stamped their loads with the date they were sterilized.

For some odd reason, the guy from Central Office in Washington, D.C., Bobby Osbourne, that oversaw everything in Sterile Processing, thought all items were time-related. Time-related meant that instead of items being sterile unless something comprised them, they were only good for a certain amount of time, either one month or one year. Peel packs, all trays, and certain items that were heat-sealed fell under the one-year time frame, everything else was one month. Everything was going well, or so I thought, a few months into the job there were a few people that treated me like crap for absolutely no reason. Sadly, I wasn't alone as a few of my coworkers were getting the same treatment by those same people. There was one big mistake that I made with them, the mistake being that I let those people get inside my head to the point where it changed me as a person.

The next summer my friend Joel Brewton and I had been looking at a few two-bedroom apartments to move into together and after several weeks of looking, we found one in Greenfield which is a suburb of Pittsburgh, PA. The place we rented looked more like a house than an apartment complex. Things were still going bad for me at my job to the point where every single day or night that I got home, I would either go into isolation by staying in my room with my door closed or get angry and take my frustrations out on my roommate. After a while enough was enough and I couldn't take it anymore. Two days in a row, upon arriving home, the first thing that happened was that I drank two shots of whiskey. Joel saw the shot glass in the sink on both days and talked to me, telling me I needed to stop what I was doing. He was really worried about me and quite frankly so was I. Before that happened, there were days that when I drank and there were depressing things that I would say. To this day the big life lesson that I learned was drinking won't make your problems go away, it will only make them worse. If I got the chance to go back and change the way I handled things, there would be a lot of changes made. In my opinion there was no excuse for my behavior. Joel was trying to help me out and instead of letting him I just kept pushing him away. When I was around other people, they had no idea what was going on because I put on a smile to hide what was happening.

In October 2009, my mom and I went on a trip together to southern California for a few days. We flew out of Pittsburgh on the fourth and had a layover at the Chicago's O'Hare Airport, which was a long walk to get to our connecting gate for the rest of the flight to San Diego. We got breakfast at the airport and then boarded the plane. After boarding, we waited a while and were told there was a problem with the fuel line which ended up causing the plane to depart an hour later than the original scheduled time of 7:45 AM. We arrived in San Diego at 11:45 AM West Coast Time. After getting our luggage, we were transported by van to the rental car place Fox Rent-a-Car. The first place we visited was the Horton Plaza to take lessons on how to ride a segway, which I caught onto quickly. Next, we took a cruise on the San Diego Bay. While on the cruise, we got to see the Coronado Island and the bridge leading to the island. To end our first night, we checked into LaJolla Inn, which didn't have a parking lot for the hotel. Instead, the car had to be parked two blocks away. The Pittsburgh Steelers was playing the San Diego Chargers that night, so my mom and I ate at the Prospect Bar and Grill which was a sports bar. I wore my Troy Polamalu jersey to the restaurant and to my surprise none of the Chargers fans there made a big deal of it and were very nice.

Monday morning we woke up early because we were going to visit the San Diego Zoo. The exit to get off for the Zoo was very confusing with it being one of those exits having the exit number followed by "A" or "B". My mom got off the wrong exit which upset me but it shouldn't have. Finally, after twenty minutes, we were able to arrive at the zoo and spent most of the day there. The world-famous panda exhibit was bigger than I expected. Later that evening on the way to dinner, there was another adventure during the car ride. My mom was trying to find a CVS Pharmacy and during the ride we passed by Petco Park, the stadium where the San Diego Padres play. After driving by the outside of it three various times we found the CVS. Once again, we had dinner and checked into our next hotel for our last night in San Diego. Before calling it a night, I went over the directions with my mom to our next destination, Burbank, and put the directions in the GPS.

Wednesday morning we got picked up by a van at the Coast Anabelle Hotel in Burbank to take us on a bus tour around Los Angeles to sightsee the different areas such as Beverly Hills. One of the things that I wanted to do on the trip was to see the Conan O'Brien and Jay Leno shows. Wednesday evening we saw Conan which was fun. The following morning on our final day of the trip, my mom and I got up early to get in line for tickets to the Jay Leno Show. That afternoon before going to the Tonight Show, we went on the Warner Brothers Studio tour which was a wonderful experience. The tour began with seeing the coffee shop set on the T.V. show *Friends* and got to sit in the studio where *Two and a Half Men* and *Big Bang Theory* were filmed and got to see both sets as well. During the tour, there were portions of it where you weren't allowed to take pictures. The tour guide told us, "Security will put you in time out."

The Jay Leno Show was the very last thing we did on the trip. There was a guy walking around the audience to scout out a fan who was really into the show that laughed at all the jokes and applauded them as well. Gerard Butler was the main draw of the show that night and during the show, some of the audience members got to go outside and see Gerard drive a racecar and timed how long it took him to complete him to complete the course. After the show was over, I felt a tap on my shoulder, turned around, and standing there was the guy from earlier in the show with a couple prizes in his hands, one was a Jay Leno Show mini-towel and other prizes I got to choose from. The guy was impressed with my audience participation and that's why he offered me the prizes. The prize I chose was the mini-towel.

Thursday October 15, 2009, after arriving home from work, I received some terrible news. My roommate had a shocked look on his face as if something bad happened to someone. He said, "Gary's dead." Gary Baker was our friend in ACE who was an Assistant Regional Rep for the Western PA region. I met Gary at CoasterBash in March 2005. At the beginning of the event, Regional Rep Bill Linkenheimer made the announcement, "If you have a cellphone, please turn it on vibrate mode or off completely. Should you answer your phone, please go outside and talk." After the announcement, Gary answered his phone and was talking on it. Bill asked Gary, "Gary, what did I just say about the cell phones?" After that, Bill proceeded to pull out a roll of duct tape and taped Gary's mouth shut, so he wouldn't be disruptive and everyone in attendance laughed about it. Later that night at the end of the event, I went to claim my door prize from Gary. I talked to him a little bit while he was getting my door prize ready. He was one of those people that you could instantly like. KennyKon was the other ACE Western PA event held in the summertime at Kennywood Park which Gary attended as well. KennyKon XX was the last time that I would get to interact with him, not knowing what would happen a few months later. For Kennywood's Halloween event Phantom Fright Nights, the ACERS that attended got to ride the wooden roller coaster the Racer that Gary was the ride operator for when he worked at Kennywood during the summer season. People that couldn't attend the funeral could go online and write their own eulogy that would be read out loud. My eulogy said, "Gary was one of the most down-to-earth people I ever met. CoasterBash, KennyKon, and CoasterCon won't be the same without you. Rest in peace, you'll be missed."

The following June, Kennywood was the host park for CoasterCon with Idlewild, Conneaut Lake, and Waldameer being the other parks. One of the activities for CoasterCon every year is the Midway Olympics in which teams of five compete against each other at the games in the midway of the park. During signups, I was the team captain and the other four members were Tim Michalak, Joel Brewton, Taz Cates, and Ken Riling. The team name that I came up with was WolfPac. Joel didn't like the name so he came up with ACE Pac. Taz and I got the two highest scores on Skee-Ball while Ken used a backspin technique and got us a score on the game where you had to land a ping-pong ball inside a glass cup. Before we headed to the last two parks of Con, that Wednesday night was the annual CoasterCon banquet. The teams with the tree highest scores from the Olympics were awarded bronze, silver, and gold medals. Two teams tied for third, one for second, with the anticipation coming of who won the gold. Joel, Ken, and I were sitting at our Banquet table whenever Bill Linkenheimer announced the team name that took first place. He said, "In first place with an unoriginal team name, ACE Pac." It took a few seconds to sink in that we won. Joel got up from his seat and said, "Wait, that's us". After hearing the bronze and silver winners, we didn't think we were going to win a medal. One night in August 2010, after all the abuse and nasty things a couple of my co-workers were doing to me, I finally reached my breaking point and threatened to commit suicide in front of my roommate, Joel. Here is how the conversation went:

Me: I am going to drink this entire bottle of Jack Daniels
Joel: That could kill you.
Me: I do not care.

If anyone out there in their life gets to that point where they want to end it, please reach out to a Friend, Family Member, or seek professional help and tell them what is going on. That is something I wish I would have done. Looking back on it, I am glad that I did not make that decision to go through with it. Over the years, I met a lot of people mainly in ACE and made new Friends as well as getting to travel to new places that I had not been to before. By the beginning of 2011, I was in a much better place and things started to get a lot better for me.

CoasterCon 34 the following year was held in Arlington, Texas, which was my very first trip to Texas. After gathering up my materials from the Con Packet. I met another ACER for the first time, Danny

Barnes and I drove to and took a tour of the Dallas Cowboys stadium. We got to walk around the stadium, then around on the field and get your picture taken on it or buy a football to toss around or try to kick a field goal. 2011 was the fiftieth anniversary of Six Flags Over Texas. To celebrate, the show included the Dallas Cowboys Cheerleaders concluding the show with fireworks. Next stop was the post-con events held in San Antonio at SeaWorld, Six Flags Fiesta Texas, and Schlitterbahn in New Brunsfel. Schlitterbahn is a big outdoor water park separated into three different sections that could only be reached by a bus provided by the park. My favorite park of the post–con events was Six Flags Fiesta Texas. Schlitterbahn was where I met Jeff Seibert.

My cousin Kaitlyn got married in the summer of 2011 in New Jersey. My parents and I drove up the day before and had a tough time finding our way to the hotel, mainly because the one road we had to take in New Jersey was closed due to construction. Finally, after a while, we arrived and had dinner at the hotel. After dinner, I went to the exercise room to work out. Somehow I smacked my glasses off a piece of equipment and bent them. Luckily, there was a place down the road from the hotel that fixed and repaired glasses. Kaitlyn's wedding took place outside and it was a nice summer day to have a wedding. It ended up raining about halfway through the reception for a while and even again at the end of it.

My Aunt Lauren and Uncle Bill held a little party at their house the next morning with most of the relatives and their son-in-law's parents as well. Everyone stayed for a while then left. As soon as my parents and I were getting ready to leave, the newlyweds, Kaitlyn and her husband Matt, showed up to the house. Kaitlyn came over to our car and said goodbye to all three of us before we headed back home.

In November, I took my first trip to Hilton Head, South Carolina and Savanah, Georgia with my parents. On the way down we stopped and stayed a couple of days with my Aunt Terina and Uncle Dan. I hadn't seen either of them since Andrea's wedding. Hilton Head wasn't that far from my aunt and uncle's place. We left on a Sunday morning and made good time. The place we stayed at was a time share not far from the beach. Walking or renting a bicycle were the two ways to get around for the most part but going to the grocery store required driving to and from. Dolphin watching was one of the activities to do in Hilton Head. A tour guide took people out on a little boat and some of the dolphins weren't too far from the boat. The tour guide said occasionally that some dolphins would come up right next to the boat but that didn't happen the day my parents and I went. Savanah, Georgia was an hour away from Hilton Head. We did a trolley ride around town and did some walking around as well. Part of the trolley ride drove past the bench in the park where some of the movie *Forrest Gump* was filmed at. Later that day we went to a museum in downtown Savanah and watched a short film about the history of the town. A couple of days later, we left Hilton Head and headed back home.

One night in the summer of 2012, after an ACE event at Idlewild, a few of us went to the Hollywood Theatre in Pittsburgh to view a midnight screening of *Rocky Horror Picture Show*. It was a tradition that had been going on at other theaters years before where people would yell things at the screen and throw different props at it. Some of the props included hot dogs and toast and the theaters decided to outlaw them after a while. It was the first time I had ever seen the movie, although there were bits and pieces I'd seen before. Jason Ballard had done midnight screenings of it before and gave me a heads up of what to expect. At the very beginning of the film, everyone in the theatre got up and did the dance to the opening song of the movie, "The Time Warp". *Rocky Horror* ended around 2 AM. Joel, Adam Carlini, and I got back to our apartment and had to get up early the next morning for KennyKon. Five hours of sleep was all we got that night. I'm still surprised we were able to get up early on such little amount of sleep. I ended up taking a little power nap during dinner time.

In the fall, I traveled to Colorado to visit Kaitlyn and Matt in Boulder with Denver being the closest airport to fly into. On our first day together, the three of us went hiking for a few hours followed by dinner at a brewery and then I checked into my hotel. Elitch Gardens is an amusement park in Denver that I hadn't been to before. It was a chance for me to show Kaitlyn and Matt what it was like in the day of a coaster enthusiast. They had a lot of fun riding everything. Matt didn't want to ride the Droptower, so Kaitlyn and I rode it instead. The last day I was there, Kaitlyn and I went on a tour of a brewery followed by everyone on the tour group going to a backroom with different beers to sample. That evening the three of us ate dinner at the same place we did the first day then went for a walk. Next morning was my flight back home to Pittsburgh. The days went by too fast.

Upon arriving home, the next day my friend and I went to a gathering done through the website *Match.com*. That was the second Match event I'd been to and had struck out at both. That week's vacation ended with me driving to Knoebel's Amusement Park for their Halloween event Phoenix Phall Phunfest, my third one in a row. Phoenix Phall Phunfest was very cold that day with temperatures in the 40s.

After living together for nearly four years, "the Crewton era," as Joel dubbed it, came to an end. He got his own place with me living in our two-bedroom apartment until the lease was up. The second apartment we lived in was a further commute to my job compared to the one in Greenfield. Part of me missed the short commute to work, so Squirrel Hill was my next place of residence in a small studio apartment. One problem with the apartment complex was parking. It was street parking and depending on what shift I was on, unless it was daylight, the only option was to park on the next street over and walk to my apartment. While I enjoyed the short commute into the city, after one year my decision was to not renew my lease. North Versailles is currently the city I'm living in now with a decent-sized one-bedroom apartment close to my parents, grocery stores, and a movie theater.

At Six Flags Over St. Louis for CosterCon 39, the very first day on Facebook my post was that I had a surprise for everyone. Throughout the day, people commented on the post and other people that day asked me what the surprise was. About a week before convention, I asked my good friend Ron Gaston, who I met at the 2011 Con, if he would be my ride partner for my milestone 200th Coaster. That's what the surprise was, that I was going to hit a milestone with it being The Boss, the park's big wooden coaster. Ron rode with me and I'm glad he got to share that moment with me. On the last day at Six Flags St. Louis, after all the activities were done, a few of us drove to Downtown St. Louis to go explore and went inside the St. Louis Arch to the top for some sightseeing. We were up there for a while looking around at the different sites below and taking photos. The two guys that I was carpooling with, Joe and Paul, got lost on the way back to our hotel and were able to get back on the correct route after a few minutes, arguing the entire way back. By the time, the three of us got back, it gave me more time than I thought to change into my dress clothes for the banquet. My good friend Maggie Altman won the PTC Award that night, which is given to an ACE Member that goes above and beyond and she deserved to win it for everything she's done for ACE.

New Year's Eve 2016, instead of doing my usual tradition of going to see a movie followed by dinner, I drove down to Weirton, West Virginia to my friend Jason's house. Jason, his fiancée Renee, and I went over to our friend Josh Brinkley's house to party and also to surprise Josh for his milestone birthday on New Year's Day. Luckily, Josh had no idea and was very surprised to receive birthday gifts from everyone. A few hours later everyone went home.

Part of Jason's bachelor party was held at King's Island for the Coasterstock event. The rest of it was held at Pinball, PA. That night a bunch of us rode in a limousine to the arcade place, played games there for a few hours, and then got back in the limousine. Nobody was in a hurry to get back to the hotel and the limo driver asked us if we wanted to go into the city. We all said yes and ended up hanging out at the Mount Washington overlook for a while and then decided to call it a night.

Once again, the next morning, the wedding party and I took a ride in a limousine to the church. Between the end of the wedding to the time the reception began, there was a lot of time to kill. To pass the time, some ACERS from the wedding went to Basil's Sports Bar and Grill just down the road, a few minutes away from the church. By the time we got back to the hotel, the reception was just about ready to begin. Their reception was different than any other one I've been to. The DJ that Jason hired played only one slow song and the rest were faster-paced ones. The whole weekend was a wonderful experience celebrating with friends along with the bride and groom, Jason, and Renee. They both did an excellent job planning their big day.

Next up was another trip to Texas for CoasterCon XL edition with Six Flags Fiesta Texas being the Host Park. Two years prior at CoasterCon 38 in New Jersey we knew about it. Jeff Filicko, who works at Fiesta Texas, came up with the idea to host the Con. Before working there, he was the public relations guy at Kennywood Park. The night before Coastercon started, my friend Eric Clevinger and I went exploring to the Alamo and the San Antonio Riverwalk. The San Antonio Riverwalk was a lot of fun to walk around, mainly because of all the restaurants and shops that were around. We walked around for a few hours checking out everything before leaving and heading back to our hotels. In my opinion, this Con was better than the other ones I attended, because of all the activities that Fiesta Texas provided for us. Dinner the first night was held in the middle of their Go-Kart track, something that hadn't been done before. We also got VIP seating for their fireworks show title Celebrate Summer Night Spectacular held outdoors. For our last day at Fiesta Texas, the park did something that no other host park at other Cons I attended had done before this one. Not only did the park give us every ride for nighttime ERT, they also let us preview two of their haunted attractions. Jeff Filicko and Jeff Seibert went out of their way for ACE at the park and did an excellent job hosting.

Seaworld San Antonio and ZTD's amusement park were the other parks included for Con. Early evening the day we were at Seaworld, about sixty ACERS left the park to go on the San Antonio Riverwalk Boat Cruise. Tickets for the Cruise got bought online as part of the registration process. It sold out in less than two days. The cruise had two boats that sat thirty people in each one with a tour guide and a bartender as well. It lasted about an hour. Following that, some people went back to SeaWorld while a lot had dinner reservations at the Riverwalk.

Finally, it was on to ZTD's, a small, family-owned amusement park, for the conclusion of CoasterCon XL. For me, that was my very first visit to the park, which was fun. The park consisted of the coaster, switchback, a Go-Kart track that went up a hill and came back down instead of your typical flat track, and some other small rides as well. After lunch, most people went back to the hotel to get ready for the banquet while some stayed a little longer and hung out at the water park.

Harry Sykes, Ron Gaston, John Gasper, and I left the park around four to go to the Riverwalk. The four of us walked around trying to decide on a place to eat. After a few minutes, we ate at Charlie Wants a

Burger Sports Bar. Dirty Nelly's Irish Pub ended up being my last stop in Texas that night. Before the four of us left, John made a toast, saying, "To CoasterCon XL edition".

Friday morning I left the hotel to go to the airport for my flight back home to Pittsburgh. Time, as it always does, go by too quickly. That week was a blast spent with great friends.

PART 5

NEW THINGS/MORE ADVENTURES

A few months into 2018, I started to take Music Lessons again, this time it was for something new that I had never thought of doing before. On April 4th, I contacted this Music Studio down the road from where I live. Guitar Performance Systems was the name of the place, I sent out an email and received one back from Dave, the owner of the place. Dave relayed the message to Chris Pickering, the guy that I was going to be taking Voice Lessons from. Prior to then taking Voice Lessons was something I never thought of doing before and wanted to try something new. At first, it was difficult, however as time went on, I got better and better at it. The first thing Chris had me do was teach me warmup exercises as well as different techniques to get my voice ready for singing different songs. The songs I would practice were Heavy Metal Songs form different bands. Those songs were not in my vocal range and at times could be difficult for me to sing, so I would get frustrated easily. Whenever that would happen, he would tell me to relax and overtime I would start to improve, which I did. After a while, I decided to start singing County Songs with singers that sang in my vocal range and that made things a lot easier. At the beginning of May, I flew down with several people from the ACE Western PA region to St. Louis the day before Spring Con took place in Branson, Missouri at the Amusement Park, Silver Dollar City. The night before the 1st day of Con, a bunch of us drove to this restaurant called Lamberts Café. What made this restaurant great was the servers would throw Dinner Rolls at the people eating there and you had to catch them. After eating there, we drove to our Hotel for the next 4 nights. During the 1st day of Spring Con, the 1st ride we went on was the parks new Roller Coaster, Time Traveler. Also, that 1st night the park gave us a nice variety of food items and desserts for Dinner, we also were the 1st group of people to get a night ride on Time Traveler. The 2nd day, we got to do some behind the scenes tours of a couple of rides and in the evening a bunch of us got to go on the Showboat Branson Belle Cruise Boat that featured entertainment with different songs being sung by the performers on the boat. The last day in Branson, a few of us went out to eat at a 50's Diner to celebrate Ken's Birthday. By the end of 2018, I was considering getting Lasik Surgery done to correct my vision, so I would not have to wear glasses anymore. I went to TLC Laser Eye Centers in Sewickley, PA to get tests done to see if I could let Lasik surgery done. Unfortunately, there was something wrong with part of my Left Eye that prevented me from that happening. An alternative option to Lasik was another form of it known at PK Surgery. PK surgery was a longer recovery time and the way the procedure was done was different. That same day I decided not to have the surgery. In late January 2019, after thinking about it for a few weeks, I changed my mind and decided to have the procedure done. It was one of the best decisions I made, and I felt like a new person afterwards. In April my Mom, Dad, and I drove down to South Carolina for the wedding of my Cousin Dylan Cronin and his Wife, Lauren. The wedding took place at the Ryan Nichols Inn in Simpsonville, South Carolina. The location used to be a house at one time, afterwards different members of the Family got pictures taken with the Bride and Groom right outside of the front entrance, while all the other guests went out back to the area where the reception was taking place. My parents and I as well as my Cousins, Katie, Austin, and my Aunt Terina got our photo taken with Dylan and Lauren. A couple of months later, I flew out for my 2nd visit to Southern California for CoasterCon 42. Prior to the 1st day of that event, I arrived a few days early and flew into Burbank. After getting my rental car, I drove to Anaheim and went to Disneyland for my very 1st visit to the Park. Upon arriving, I contacted my friends Adam Napotnik, his Mom Tina, and Adam Carlini to see where they were at. After a while I ran into them and we hung out for most of the day. Later that night I left for the Hotel I was staying at for my other visit to Universal Studios Hollywood. The next day I went to Universal Studios Hollywood and had a good time there and because I was by myself, I got to take advantage of the single rider line, and hardly had any wait time to ride certain rides, even though the park was busy that day. The day before CoasterCon 42 started, my friends Joel Brewton, Ken Riling, and I rode down to the Santa Monica Pier to hang out for several hours. We walked around the Pier as well as the surrounding area and ended the day there by riding the Roller Coaster. Over the course of the next several days during CoasterCon 42 I got to experience my 1st visits to both Six Flags Magic Mountain and Knotts Berry Farm. Both parks did a good job with the Convention and I really enjoyed my visit to both Parks. After Con was over it was time for the Post Con events. The Friday after Con was over was at a small family park, Castle Park which had a nice little Coaster, Mini Golf Course, and an indoor shoot in the dark game. After leaving Castle Park, that same day my roommate for the Con as well as the Add On events and my friend, Mark met up at the Hotel we were staying at and rode down together to Belmont Park in San Diego. Belmont Park is located on a Boardwalk near a beach, so there were rides as well as other things to do. The main attraction was their Roller Coaster, Giant Dipper. After riding that a few times I met up with my Friends, Jes, her husband Kyle, her brother Jeff, Adam Napotnik and Adam Carlini. We hung out a little bit and rode some of the other rides. Following that Mark and I were watching a performance in the middle of the Boardwalk by a woman named, Hillia Hula. She was performing different acts with her Hula Hoops, something I had never seen done before. After the performance Mark and I talked to Hillia a little bit as well as getting a picture taken with her. The last park of the Add on days was at Sea World San Diego. During my visit there, the park gave us morning ERT, Lunch which during you could get a picture taken with a Penguin named Pete as well as a Shark Mascot. After lunch, a few friends and I rode some rides and saw a show. My last day in Southern California I checked out of the Hotel, my roommate and I had breakfast, and then I drove back to the Burbank Airport for my flight back home to Pittsburgh, PA. My second trip to California was a blast and I enjoyed it more than my 1st visit there in 2009. Later that summer besides Voice Lessons. I started to take Guitar Lessons as well from the Same instructor. I have been learning to play some different songs as well as songs from Mel Bay's Modern Guitar Method Grade 1 and after playing from that book for over a year, I moved on to Mel Bay's Modern Guitar Method Grade 2. The year 2019 was a great year for me. My Journey has been one full of ups and downs, such is life. There has been a lot of great memories I've made throughout the years and I'm looking forward to making many more plus seeing what the future holds for me.

THANK YOU'S/DEDICATION

Thank you to the following people:

First and foremost, to my parents for being so patient with me growing up. Your unconditional love and support means more to me then you'll ever know.

Ryan Oreski, my best friend of twenty-five and a half years, hard to believe we've known each other that long.

The Teen Group, it's great to see how far we've all come in fifteen years. I'm glad you're all my friends.

American Coaster Enthusiasts, there's so many people I've met in that club over the years. Too many people to name, I don't want to leave anyone out. It's always great to see everyone at all the events.

This book is dedicated to the Memory of Ken Riling.

Thank You for all the Roller Coaster Adventures we have shared as well as your 10 plus years of Friendship.

www.ingramcontent.com/pod-product-compliance
Lightning Source LLC
Chambersburg PA
CBHW051553120626
46551CB00013B/1491